Title & Copyright

UNFUCK YOUR CREDIT UPDATED 2019

Glen Whitten

ISBN: 9781728890418

Dedication

This book is dedicated to all of the hard-working men and women who are just trying to make a life for themselves and their families. I have been in your shoes and I feel your pain. This book is for you.

CONTENTS

Foreword

What's the first thing you think of when someone says they need to see your credit report? If you're like most people, your first impulse is to start making a few excuses.

- I went through a divorce
- I had a business fail
- I had some medical issues
- I was laid off/unemployed

The funny thing is that in my experience, the person asking is typically not judging you. They are usually sympathetic because, you guessed it; they have the same issues in their credit file.

Most people, no matter what their credit looks like, wish their credit score was higher. According to recent statistics, 56% of consumers have poor credit. That's right--more than one out of every two adults in this country have bad credit.

So there you have it. If you know more than two people, odds are at least half of them have bad credit. You are not alone. In fact, you are in the majority. Not that it makes you feel better, but with these kinds of staggering numbers, you can be sure that there's no shame in it. Being ashamed of your past issues and mistakes is just plain crazy.

If something is affecting half the population and no one ever talks about it, it will never get fixed. That's why we are here. We are helping people take back the control and get back on top financially.

In the past, you not only couldn't see your credit file, you weren't even *allowed* to know your credit score or how it was calculated. The good news is your government has opened the door to let these millions of consumers in on the biggest secret since Roswell or the Kennedy assassination.

You, the consumer, can finally access your credit file for free and you can repair your own credit, also for free. You don't need a lawyer, a college degree or a credit counseling company to guide you through the red tape. You can do it yourself and you can do it for free.

The credit bureaus are *legally* obligated to show you your credit report for free. Also, they are *legally* obligated to remove negative items from your credit report if they can't verify them in 30 days or less.

Take a look through the rest of the material here and make a plan, but most of all, get started. Watch your credit score climb out of the basement. Start reaping the benefits that have only belonged to the few who had access to this process.

TAKE Your credit back!!!

CHAPTER ONE

Effects of bad credit on your life

Now that we know half of Americans have poor credit, let's look at why exactly that's such a big deal.

If you watch any crime shows, one of the phrases you hear when discussing why someone was murdered is "Follow the money." The same is true here. Why would having low credit scores be a problem? What does your credit score cost you in life?

Money costs money when you borrow it and if you have a low credit score, you are considered a higher risk. Being a higher risk means you will either be denied or will pay a *lot* more to borrow that money.

First off, it's almost impossible to get a home loan if you have a low credit score. Banks are in the business of making money with money. You put your money in a bank and they loan it out to someone else and charge them interest until the money is paid back. That's a little bit simplified, but you get the idea.

If your credit score is low, you probably won't qualify for a home loan and if you do, you're going to have to put down a very large down payment and pay a high interest rate. All of that just means that if you have a low credit score, you'll probably be renting.

> *Bottom line, you will likely never own a home until you fix your credit score.*

* * *

And what about that place you're renting? You may not even be able to rent a place to live depending on your credit and where you want to live. Most reputable landlords run credit reports before letting you agree to pay 100% interest to live there.

I don't necessarily blame them, but it makes things really tough on someone who has fallen on hard times and has to move out of their home. What if they can't find anyone to rent them another place to live?

If you do find a place to rent, I can just about promise you that the landlord will require a much higher deposit if you have poor credit.

Next, you will definitely pay higher interest rates on your credit cards and other loans. That means that people who probably already can't afford things are now going to be able to afford less once they pay all that extra interest.

It's a crazy spiral. You have poor credit so you can't get a new car. You end up paying higher interest for a used car. The higher payment means you have to buy a car that could end up costing you even more money in repairs.

That used car also won't last as long and will be worth less when you go to sell it or trade it. What's worse is you likely paid as much over time as someone with good credit paid (with much lower interest) for a new car. Starting to see the problem?

Here's another catch 22: you have bad credit because you couldn't pay your bills after you lost your job. Evidently someone has a great sense of humor since these days it's not uncommon for employers to run a credit check on you before they agree to hire you. Thankfully there are still employers out there who don't, but you won't know until you apply. Your dream job could be out of reach for you based on your credit score.

Let's say you do get that job and you do find a place to live. How about when you go to sign up for utilities? Utility companies (water, gas, electricity, cable, etc.) usually run a credit check prior to letting you sign up for service. If they don't like what they see, you could be required to put down a hefty deposit before they will allow you to set up service.

When you are moving, this could be a serious burden in addition to your rent, deposit and moving costs. It doesn't even matter if you've never been late on your utilities in your life--if you have low credit scores, they will probably ask for that deposit.

Ever tried to sign up for one of those great cell phone deals offered by the major wireless companies? Unfortunately those deals are for people with good credit only. If your score doesn't meet their requirements, you will not get that deal and may even have to get a high priced prepaid service.

So now you've found a job, found a place to rent, bought a car and somehow set up all your utilities. Get ready for the next bomb to go off. Insurance companies also check your credit before issuing a quote or a policy. In some cases, if your score is too low, they will deny you service or require a co-applicant. In most cases, they just charge you more--a LOT more for the same coverage as someone with good credit. I don't understand it either, but the law allows them to charge you more for the same coverage so they do.

Finally, bad credit means you probably owe money to people and that means stress. LOTS of stress. Bills coming in every day, credit collection agencies calling you and sending you letters and worst of all, judgments and liens and garnishments.

The bottom line is that it feels like when you're down, they just keep kicking. Why do they do this? Because they can and because all those fees, deposits and interest payments add up to BILLIONS of dollars. Buy here/pay here, rent to own, payday loans, title loans and pawn shops all make their money on the people who can least afford it.

Get off the treadmill and get out of the financial hole by fixing your credit and paying less.

CHAPTER TWO

Basics of credit repair

Fixing your own credit is not only your right, it's free and it's easy. If you like, you can read the Fair Credit Reporting Act for yourself, but here is the boiled down version.

There are lots of credit reporting companies (aka credit bureaus), but the big three are Equifax, Transunion and Experian. Almost anyone pulling your credit will go to one or more of these three.

Credit reporting companies make their money by gathering information about you. They keep a very detailed file on you and always have. They track your name, address, employer, loans, payment history, credit cards, credit inquiries (loan/credit card applications) and lots more.

Throughout your adult life, when you apply for credit, a lease, a job, etc, the bureaus then sell your information to where ever you applied. Those companies pay the credit bureaus to give them a snapshot of your credit history.

These lenders and service providers who pull your credit are really only interested in your ability and likelihood to pay them on time. In the case of an employer, they are looking to see whether or not you are trustworthy. If your credit file is good, you get what you want. If it's bad you might not get what you want. If you do get it--you will have to pay more for it.

* * *

For many years, that's how things went. If you had bad credit information (even if it wasn't accurate) you didn't get what you wanted. The bad part is no one had to tell you why. You just got denied and that was it. In other words, there was very little accountability.

Eventually the FCRA (Fair Credit Reporting Act) came along and gave consumers some very important rights. Most importantly you are now entitled to:

1) A free complete copy of your credit file from all three major credit bureaus every year.

2) The right to have any information in your credit file formally investigated to verify it's accuracy.

3) The right to have any inaccurate information corrected or deleted.

4) The requirement that if the bureaus can't verify the information within 30 days--they must delete it from your credit file.

What all this means is that you can now fix your credit for free and the credit bureaus legally have to help you do it. Once you access your credit file (which can do now do online), you can initiate a free investigation of any negative items (late payments, liens, judgments, bankruptcies, collections, etc.).

The credit bureaus have to contact the creditors of any items you disputed and ask them to verify the accuracy of each piece of information. If the creditor finds a mistake and reports it back to the bureau within 30 days, the credit bureau will update your file and notify you.

However, if the creditor doesn't respond within 30 days, the credit bureau BY LAW must remove that negative item from your credit report.

Finally, if they creditor does respond and verifies the negative information, it stays on your report until it falls off (usually 7-10 years).

* * *

The best news is that if it doesn't get removed the first time you dispute it, you can repeat the process as many times as you like until it does get removed.

The process laid out in this book will step you through the process in a couple of different ways—each with a different goal. If you want fast results, but are not necessarily concerned with maximizing your score, use the online dispute. If you are looking for maximum impact and are not in a huge hurry, use the letter approach.

However you attack your report, just remember that knowing what's in your credit report is half the battle towards improving your score. Hats off to you for taking the first step and best of luck to you as you move forward.

I'll say this again in the book, but if you ever have any questions, feel free to email me and I will personally respond. The best way to reach me is by emailing me at glenwhitten@hotmail.com. I read every email and I love getting your questions and feedback.

Last, remember that your credit probably didn't get fucked up overnight and while lots of people get dramatic results in a short time, certain items can take some effort to erase. Be patient because the credit companies are counting on you running out of steam so they don't have to deal with you any more.

It's your credit—take it back.

Let's get started!

CHAPTER THREE

How to get your free credit report

The process of repairing your credit starts with getting a peak inside your credit report. Every American, thanks to the Fair Credit Reporting Act is entitled by law to receive a free and complete copy of their individual credit report every year.

There are many ways to get your free credit report, but the one sponsored by the government is the best and most accurate way to go. This part you can do entirely online.

Start by visiting the website www.AnnualCreditReport.com. Once you are there you can request your credit files from:

Equifax http://www.equifax.com/about-equifax/company-profile
Experian http://www.experian.com/corporate/about-experian.html
TransUnion https://www.transunion.com/about-us/about-transunion

You can either order and view each copy online, or request that a copy be mailed to you.

You'll have to enter personal information and answer several security questions to verify your identity. Since you are looking at your own credit report, there will be no negative impact on your credit score. Also, this is a highly secure government run website. You can tell them whatever they want to know—they already know your underwear size anyway if believe that Snowden guy.

Take the time to print at least one copy of your report, but it may be a good idea to print several copies for your files. If you dispute items you will want a copy to refer to during the investigation and for comparison once everything is finished.

If you choose to download your copy, make sure you have up-to-date antivirus and malware protection programs. If someone steals your information during the download or from your computer, you'll have a lot more work to do!

If you decide you just aren't comfortable doing all of this over the web, you can order your free copy of your credit report by phone at 1-877-322-8228.

You can also request your file by mail, which will require you to print the order form online and mail it to the agencies with identifying information.

However you choose to get your copy, you will need that complete copy in order to start any disputes. Without it, you will be denied any attention by any of the credit bureaus and creditors.

Once you have a complete copy of your credit report from all three bureaus, you are ready to begin the process of fixing your own credit!

CHAPTER FOUR

How to fix your own credit

Now you're ready to get started. You have your complete credit report from all 3 credit bureaus and by now you have no doubt read through everything.

You are also realizing something that is pretty scary--there is a LOT of information in that file and not all of it is accurate. In fact, 1 in 5 consumers will find inaccurate information on their personal credit file. This fact is exactly why the FCRA requires the credit bureaus to honor the dispute process.

What you are about to do is take advantage of the laws that were written to protect you. No one is going to help you. The creditors and the bureaus are not going to voluntarily help you fix your credit. Why? There's a lot of money at stake here. See the chapter on the Effects Of Bad Credit On Your Life for the details.

All you really need to know right now is that the law is on your side and with a few clicks and some attention to detail, you can get started scrubbing some of those negative items off your credit report. Each time you get something negative removed, your score will likely go up.

As you look over your credit reports, you may get discouraged by the amount of items you need to attack, but don't worry. Even though this may take some time, just remember that every negative item you eliminate from your credit report will save you lots of money in the long run so it's worth the effort!

Also, if you find a negative item from one credit reporting agency, you will want to make sure you check all three bureaus and dispute that item across the board.

You can attack the credit bureaus any way you want, but for the sake of this chapter, let's go alphabetically. The process is basically the same for all three companies once you get into your report.

This information is accurate and complete as of the time this was written, but obviously things could change. If they do, don't worry because the process will likely be pretty close to what you see here.

Lets Get to it:

First, visit https://www.equifax.com/personal/disputes/

- Once you arrive there, you will click the blue button on the right side of the page that reads "start a dispute"

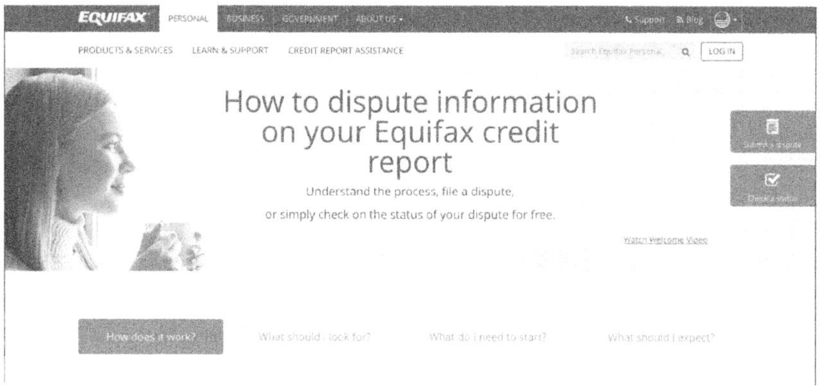

- Make sure your pop up blocker is turned off.
- A new window will pop up that starts with entering your 10-digit confirmation number.

EQUIFAX Online Dispute

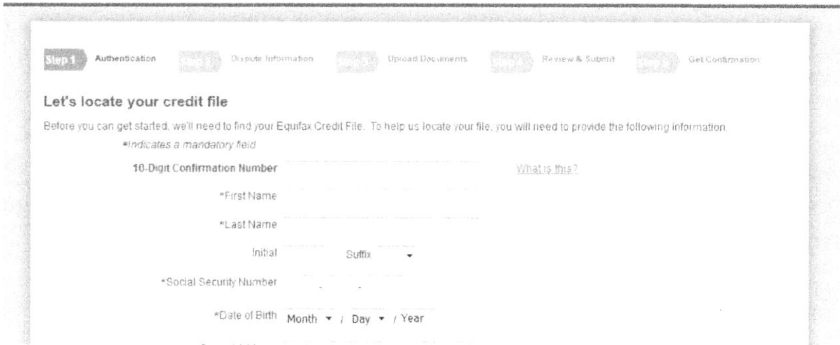

- Your 10-digit confirmation number is located on your copy of the Equifax credit report.
    - If you requested it by email, it will be in the first email they send you.
    - If you requested a copy by mail, it will be on the heading of the first page of your credit report.
- After you enter the confirmation number, you will be

prompted for several detailed pieces of personal information. This can be frustrating, but the bureau is just trying to protect your identity by making sure you are who you say you are.

- Once you get through the verification screen, you will be get to see your actual credit report.

- First things first: If you haven't already done it, make sure you print several copies of your complete credit report. You will need one clean copy for reference and at least one copy to keep track of your notes.

- Start marking the items that contain errors so you can get them corrected or removed.

- Start marking all negative items for dispute.

- Look for any missing information that could help you as well. Examples include good credit lines or cell phone bills that you have paid regularly. These may be added later with a request to the provider.

The dispute process is actually pretty straight forward. They do make minor changes regularly, but follow the steps until you reach the page where you can identify which accounts you wish to dispute.

There are several schools of thought on the best way to attack these items, but here are a some guidelines:

- Generally speaking, public records (foreclosures, liens, bankruptcies, judgments, etc) are the most damaging to your score; however, they are also some of the most difficult to remove. Start with these.

- Collections and charge offs have a significant impact on your score as well, so get to these early.

- Late payments on home & car loans should be handled next.

- Late payments on credit cards and other loans (unsecured)

will be next.

- Medical bills and pretty much anything not covered above should be dealt with last.

You could of course just dispute every negative item on your report, but beware--if you appear to be just blanket disputing all negative items, the bureau can flag your dispute as frivolous and refuse to investigate. If this happens, you will need to request another dispute investigation in writing along with a statement explaining why your request is NOT frivolous.

Obviously there are ways through this situation, but its better to avoid it in the first place by conducting several rounds of disputes over a longer period of time. Generally, once the first investigation concludes (30-45 days) you can then get a new copy of your credit report and start over.

A few notes about disputes on specific items:

- You can dispute any item on your credit report, but stick to the negative items.

- You will be asked for a reason for each dispute. If there are verifiable errors then use them. Things like:

    - Misspelled names

    - Incorrect Addresses

    - Incorrect account number

    - Incorrect balance/high balance

    - Incorrect dates for opening/closing/late payments

    - Charge off on a paid account

    - There are many others, but these are the most common

- If you have documents to back up your dispute, you may upload/mail them to support your request. Documentation is great, but certainly not required to dispute any items on your report.

- If you aren't sure what may be wrong with the account, you can simply request that ALL details of that account be verified with the original creditor. This is the most common approach.

- Any public records over 10 years old should be disputed based on their age.

- Any other records/accounts over 7 years old should be disputed based on their age.

It is generally a good idea to dispute older items when given a choice. Typically creditors move files to storage after 2 years. If this is the case, the creditor may not even bother responding to the bureau's request for verification. If the creditor chooses not to respond, that item gets removed after 30 days by law.

Remember that the creditor for a closed account (old loan, charge off, collection, etc.) has absolutely nothing to gain by taking the time to respond to the investigation. Therefore many times they don't respond. Good for you.

As you're starting to see, this process finally allows the individual consumer to use paperwork and red tape against these big companies. Most of these battles are won because the people who have to actually do the paperwork have absolutely no motivation to do the work.

Worst of all for them, there is nothing in it for them to chase paper all over just to respond to your dispute. In the end, many of these items you dispute get deleted because nobody cares enough to verify it so it falls off automatically after 30 days. It's about time the red tape works for us instead of against us!

Anyway, start with the most damaging items and work your way down. In a later chapter you will find information on how to aggressively work to remove stubborn items from your credit report, but for now let's continue.

Once you have disputed the items in this first round, you will receive email confirmation and be given a way to check on the status of your dispute. You can check on your case all you like, but the bureau will actually notify you when the investigation is completed. Nothing will update on the site or your credit report until they completely finish your investigation.

As soon as the bureau finishes their investigation, you will be able see and print the results of their investigation. As you read through the new detailed report, you will see one of three basic responses next to each of the accounts you disputed:

- The information was verified and remains the same on your credit report

- Some aspect of the information was changed, but the account remains on your credit report

- The account was deleted from your credit report

If it was deleted, pat yourself on the back because you just increased your credit score.

If a negative account remains on your credit report, don't despair--you will be given more tools later to try again.

Assuming all the negative items you disputed were removed, update the notes on your original credit report and move on to the next round of disputes. This time you will dispute the next wave of negative accounts. This process repeats itself every 30-45 days until you have attempted to remove all negative items from your credit report at least once.

At the same time you are disputing Equifax, you can also dispute the other two bureaus.

* * *

Next, let's visit Experian

Visit www.Experian.com At the home page scroll down several screens until you see the menu below. Next click on the "Disputes" button. Then click on "Start a new dispute online."

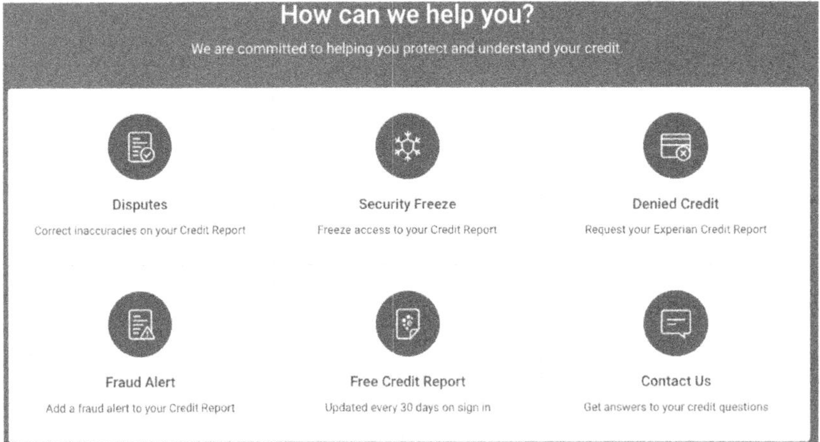

- Once you click on the "Disputes" button, you will be taken to the following page
- When you get here, look under the "How would you like to begin?" On the lower left for the "Start a new dispute online" link.

* * *

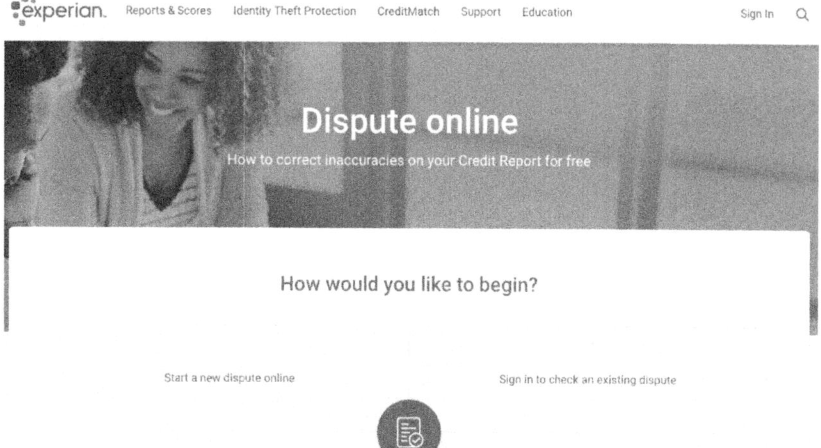

- Next, if you are new to Experian, you will need to set up a user profile.
- Start with your name, address, phone and email.
- Just follow the prompts on the screen past your SS number and date of birth all the way down until you see a purple button called "Submit and Continue like below

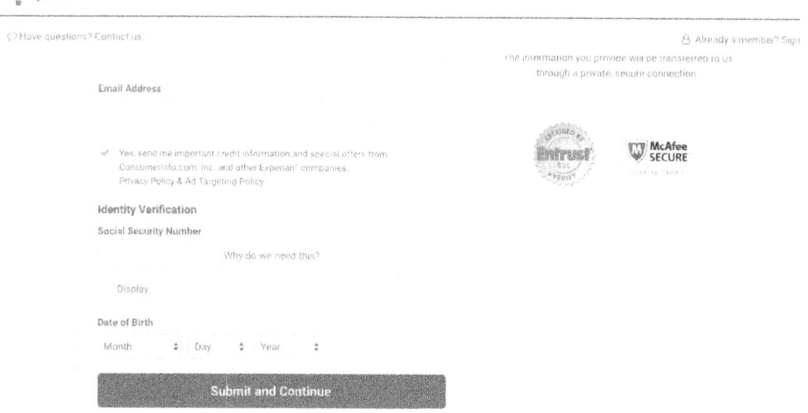

- Next you will finish setting up your profile by selecting which type of account you want (Pick the free one) and choosing your username, password, security questions and pin as shown below.

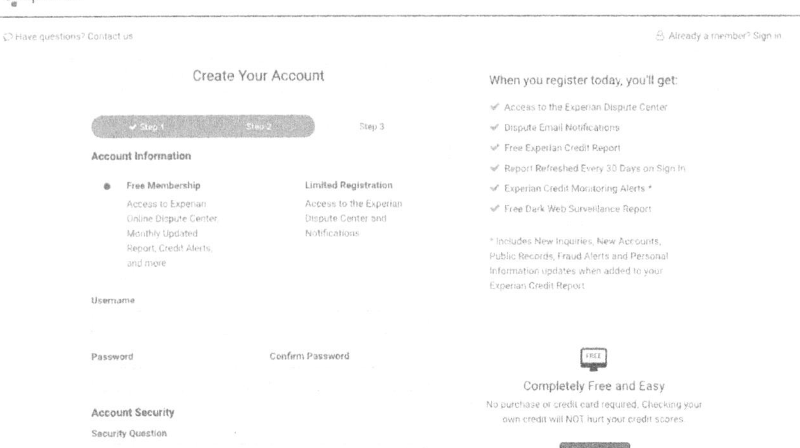

- Once you submit and Experian confirms your information you will be given a series of questions to further confirm you are who you say you are. You will have 5 minutes to answer about 3 multiple choice questions such as "Click the answer that shows the year you were born" and "Click the answer that shows the name of the high school you graduated from"
- Answer these questions and you will then see a screen where you agree to their terms and conditions.
- Check the box and click "Continue to Dispute Center" as seen here.

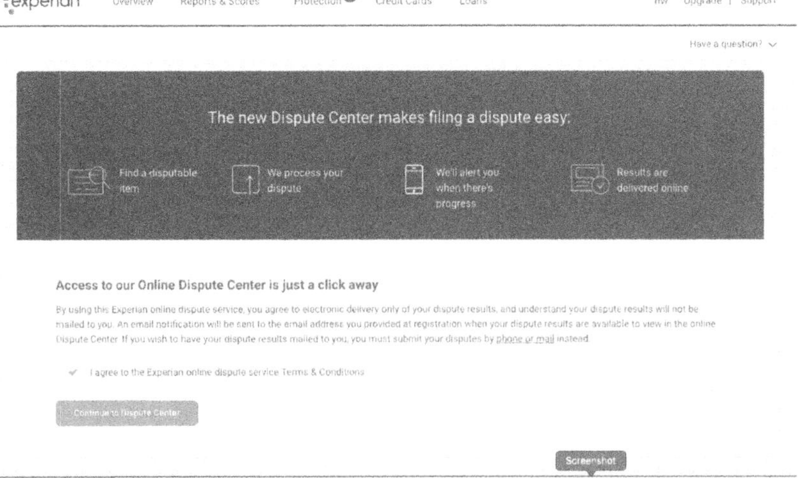

* * *

- Next you'll be in the Dispute Center main page. Click on the blue "Start a new dispute" button shown here.
-

- Once inside the Dispute Center, you will see a summary of your Experian Credit Report.
- Experian highlights on the left side, the "Potentially Negative" items on your report.
- The easiest and fastest way to get started is to click the blue "Dispute" button next to each item like you see here.

Potentially Negative

CAPITAL ONE **Dispute**

- Again, you will follow the instructions from earlier on deciding which negative items to dispute
- Read over the information and decide on the best reason to dispute the information. Click the drop down menu to see the list they give you like you see here.

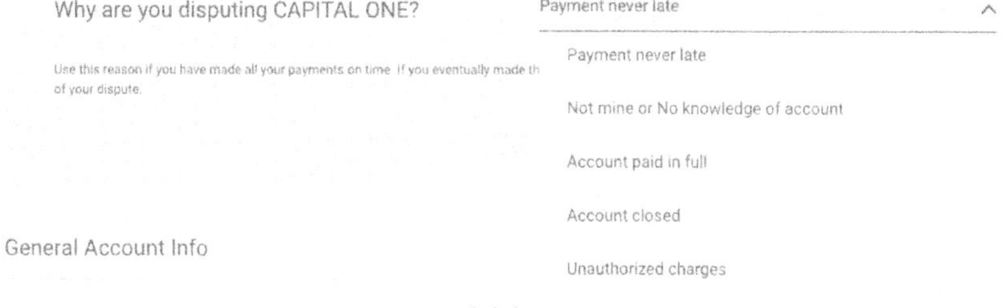

* * *

- Select your reason (if you don't see the one you like, choose one that is as close as you can.) It really doesn't matter in the end because Experian will verify all aspects of the account anyway. Then hit next.
- Next you will be allowed to comment. Do or don't, it's doubtful anyone will actually read your comments anyway.
- After this screen you will be allowed to submit your dispute.
- Again, it's about 30-45 days until you will get an email telling you that your investigation is finished

Now let's head to TransUnion

Last, visit https://www.transunion.com/credit-disputes/dispute-your-credit for the 3rd major credit bureau:

- Once here, you'll need to click the "File a credit dispute or check status now" link.

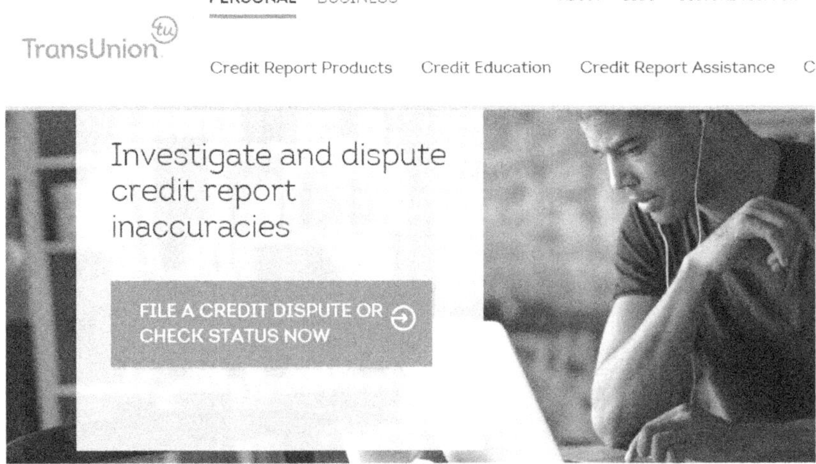

* * *

- If this is your first time on their site, you'll be asked to log in or register.

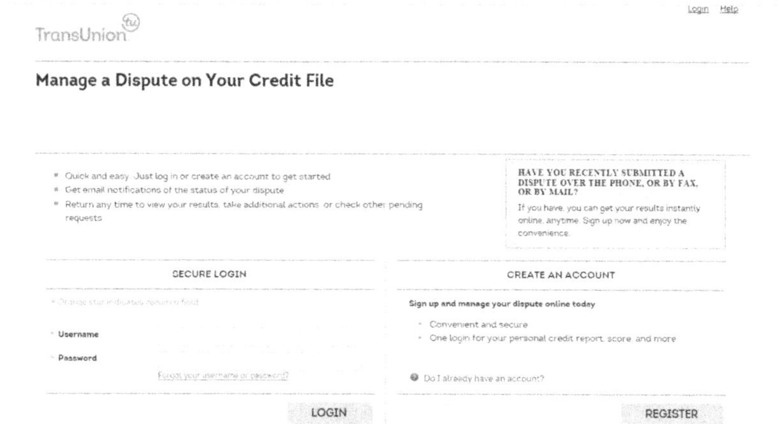

- After this, you'll be able to see your credit report and start disputing the negative items like you did with the other two bureaus.

That's it! Just a little time invested in each site will bring you fastest and easiest results you can get anywhere. All for free and all without any legal help.

You are now taking control of your credit and starting to take control of your financial health.

CHAPTER FIVE

12 Credit repair letters that work

When the online dispute methods don't eliminate all of the negative items from your report there are a few things you can do:

- Start another online dispute and repeat until all items are deleted or your attempts are flagged as frivolous (see previous chapter).

- Wait for the legal expiration date to pass and then request those items be removed (7-10 years).

- Give up and be happy for the items you did get removed.

- Get more aggressive with your efforts.

This section focuses on the last method. As they say, when the going gets tough, the tough get going. Most people don't bother sticking with things once they become more difficult. If that's you then you can go ahead and skip this chapter. Why? Because this chapter involves a little effort and some expenses at the post office.

Is it worth it? You bet it is. For the cost of some registered letters and the time it takes to write them, file them and follow up, you can actually remove most if not all of the negative items from your credit report. Imagine the money you will save in fees, interest, late payments, collection charges, deposits when you have good credit. Most people have more time than money so if you're still reading, congratulations--you're more dedicated than 90% of the people who have bad credit.

The crazy thing is that the creditors and bureaus are COUNTING on the fact that most people won't take the time to follow through on the work it takes to clean up a messy credit report. In this chapter you will get access to 12 letters that, if you write them correctly, could erase EVERY negative item from your credit reports FOREVER.

CHAPTER SIX

Basics of letter writing

Let's get started with a few notes on your upcoming letter-writing war!!

- These letters should be used in order for each set of disputes. Once the negative items are deleted/corrected, you can start over with the first letter.

- These letters should be hand written with underlines and highlights in several places of your choosing.

    - The credit bureaus use computers to read and respond to your letters.

    - Once their computers read your letters, they initiate a computer investigation to your creditors.

    - Your creditors use computers to verify and respond to the bureaus computer inquiry.

    - Hand writing letters with underlines and highlights increases the likelihood that a PERSON will actually read your letter.

    - If a person reads your letter, the whole process gets better for you.

- Once a person reads your letter, they will initiate a human investigation. Why is this good?
    - Human beings are much slower than computers (remember the 30 day deadline?)
    - Humans are more likely to make a mistake (any mistake must be fixed in your favor.)
    - Humans are more likely to be lazy and not follow through on the request.
    - A human might actually decide not to pursue your verification and just agree to delete it either at the credit bureau or the creditor.
- If a human at the creditor or the credit bureau gets a human request, they might not follow through because:
    - The files they need are in storage
    - They can't find what they need
    - They don't have time
    - They were on vacation/sick when the request came in
    - The paperwork gets lost/misdirected
    - There's nothing in it for them except more work
    - It's easier just to delete the item from your credit report than chase everything down to properly verify or investigate your dispute
- Once you have successfully gotten the first few items deleted, start the process over with the first letter
- Always send these letters by REGISTERED mail.

  - It does cost, but this is very important
  - It shows who signed for your letter
  - It shows when they signed for your letter
  - It starts the 30 day clock in a way that you can prove
  - They know they only have 30 days and that you can prove it

- Keep and file a copy of EVERYTHING:
  - The letters you send
  - Any supporting documents you send along
  - The envelop you used
  - The version of your credit report you used for reference
  - The registered letter receipts/notifications
  - Any responses you get from the creditor/credit bureau

- Keep your files organized by credit bureau and creditor

- Use a calendar to keep track of every letter you send to everyone.

- This is where most people give up. Once the filing and the trips to the post office start to add up, most people figure it's not worth it or that they will get to it later. The problem is, they never do.

- If you really want to get the tough items off your credit report and get the life you deserve by having great credit, then you will follow through.

- Set reminders on your phone calendar or find a friend who is more organized than you.

- However you get across the finish line, make sure you stick with it.

- Use the guide in the previous chapter to decide which items to attack first.

- Do not dispute more than 3 items at a time.

- If one of your 3 disputed items gets deleted, but others remain; use the next letter in the series and just remove any references to the account that was deleted.

- Once all 3 items are deleted from your credit report, you may attack the next 3 items starting with the first letter.

- Repeat this process until you are satisfied.

- Request an updated copy of your credit report each time something is removed/updated and file all your credit reports in date order.

CHAPTER SEVEN

How to use these letters

A few things about using these letters

The addresses you will use for the credit bureaus are:

Equifax Information Services LLC.
P.O. Box 740256.
Atlanta, GA 30374.

Experian
P.O. Box 4500.
Allen, TX 75013.

Transunion
Consumer Dispute Center.
P.O. Box 2000.
Chester, PA 19016

Make sure you hand write these addresses neatly on the envelopes along with your return address. Hand writing instead of computer printing increases the odds that your letter will be handled by a person rather than a computer.

Hand write the following letters using underlines and a highlighter occasionally throughout each letter. This keeps the Credit Bureaus and creditors from using computers to conduct your investigation.

A few things before you write your first letter:

- You must write neatly!!
- Each letter number is followed by a brief description of the purpose of that letter along with whether it goes to a credit bureau or a creditor.
    - Credit bureaus are Equifax, Experian & Transunion
    - Creditors are the companies that report your credit information to the bureaus.
    - Therefore if the account in question is found on your Equifax report and is about your Citibank credit card, The Credit Bureau is Equifax and the Creditor is Citibank.
- The letter numbers and descriptions in parentheses are only for your reference and are not to be included in your letters. Just start with the name of the Credit Bureau (Equifax, Experian, Transunion) or your creditor.
- Anything in brackets {...} is information you need to fill in.
- Anything with ** by it means you will include a hard copy of that item with your letter such as a copy of your credit report or a previous letter, etc.
- Once you get a response or 45 days after you send your letter, send the next letter.

Now…let's get to it.

LETTER #1

(Initial letter to Credit Bureau disputing items)

{Name of Bureau}

{Address}

{Date}

{Name on account}

{Report number}

To whom it may concern:

On {Date of Credit Report} I received a copy of my credit report which contains errors that are damaging to my credit score. I am requesting the following items be completely investigated as each account contains several mistakes.

{Creditor 1 / Account number}

{Creditor 2 / Account number}

{Creditor 3 / Account number}

Thank you in advance for your time. I understand that you need to check with the original creditors on these accounts and that you will make sure every detail is accurate. I also understand that under the Fair Credit Reporting Act you will need to complete
your investigation within 30 days of receiving this letter. Once you are finished with your investigation, please send me a copy of my new credit report showing the changes. I look forward to hearing from you as I am actively looking for a new job and wouldn't want these mistakes on my credit report to stand in my way.

* * *

Sincerely,

{Your signature}

{Your Printed Name}

{Your Address}

{Your Phone Number}

{Your Social Security Number}

Include a copy of the credit report showing which accounts you are disputing

LETTER #2

(When you don't get a response from Letter #1)

{Name of Bureau}

{Address}

{Date}

{Name on account}

{Report number}

To whom it may concern:

On {Date of your first letter} I sent you a letter asking you to investigate several mistakes on my credit report. I've included a copy of my first letter and a copy of the report with the mistakes circled. The Fair Credit Reporting Act says I should only have to wait 30 days for the investigation to be finished. It has been more than 30 days and I still have not heard anything.

I'm guessing that since you have not responded that you were not able to verify the information on the mistaken accounts. Since it has been more than 30 days, please remove the mistakes from my credit report and send me a copy of my updated credit report. Also, as required by law, please send an updated copy of my credit report to anyone who requested a copy of my credit file in the past six months.

I look forward to hearing from you as I am actively looking for a new job and wouldn't want these mistakes on my credit report to stand in my way.

* * *

Sincerely,

{Your signature}

{Your Printed Name}

{Your Address}

{Your Phone Number}

{Your Social Security Number}

Include a copy of the credit report showing which accounts you are disputing

Include a copy of your original letter

Include a copy of the registered letter receipts showing the date they received your original letter

LETTER #3

(Request for removal of negative items from original creditor)

{Name of Creditor}

{Address}

{Date}

{Name on account}

To whom it may concern:

On {Date of Credit Report} I received a copy of my credit report which contains errors that are damaging to my credit score. I am requesting the following items be completely investigated as each account contains several mistakes.

{Description of item(s) you are disputing/account number(s)}

I have included a copy of the credit report and have highlighted the account(s) in question.

Thank you in advance for your time. I understand that you need to check on these accounts and that you will make sure every detail is accurate. I also understand that under the Fair Credit Reporting Act you will need to complete your investigation within 30 days of receiving this letter. Once you are finished with your investigation, please alert all major credit bureaus where you have previously reported my information. Also, please send me a letter confirming the changes.

* * *

I look forward to hearing from you as I am actively looking for a new job and wouldn't want these mistakes on my credit report to stand in my way.

Sincerely,

{Your signature}

{Your Printed Name}

{Your Address}

{Your Phone Number}

{Your Social Security Number}

Include a copy of the credit report showing which accounts you are disputing

LETTER #4

(If you don't receive a response from Letter #3)

{Name of Creditor}

{Address}

{Date}

{Name on account}

To whom it may concern:

On {Date of your first letter} I sent you a letter asking you to investigate several mistakes on my credit report. I've included a copy of my first letter and a copy of the report with the mistakes circled. The Fair Credit Reporting Act says I should only have to wait 30 days for the investigation to be finished. It has been more than 30 days and I still have not heard anything.

I'm guessing that since you have not responded that you were not able to verify the information on the mistaken accounts. Since it has been more than 30 days, please immediately report the updated information to all major credit bureaus so they may update my credit report. Also, please send me a letter confirming these changes to the way you report my account.

I look forward to hearing from you as I am actively looking for a new job and wouldn't want these mistakes on my credit report to stand in my way.

* * *

Sincerely,

{Your signature}

{Your Printed Name}

{Your Address}

{Your Phone Number}

{Your Social Security Number}

Include a copy of the credit report showing which accounts you are disputing

Include a copy of your original letter

Include a copy of the registered letter receipts showing the date they received your original letter

LETTER #5

(If the Credit Bureau doesn't remove negative items disputed)

{Name of Credit Bureau}

{Address}

{Date}

{Name on account}

{Report number}

To whom it may concern:

On {Date of your first letter} I sent you a letter asking you to investigate several mistakes on my credit report. I've included a copy of my first letter and a copy of the report with the mistakes circled. According to your response you have chosen to leave these negative items on my credit report adding insult to injury. The items in question are:

{Creditor 1 / Account number}

{Creditor 2 / Account number}

{Creditor 3 / Account number}

I find it completely unacceptable that you and the creditor refuse to properly investigate my dispute. Your refusal to follow the Fair Credit Reporting Act is causing me untold stress and anxiety. Since you won't follow through, I want to know exactly how you investigated each account. Therefore I would like the name, title and contact information for the person at the creditor with whom you did the investigation.

This will allow me to personally follow up with the creditor and find out why they are choosing to report these mistakes on my credit month after month.

I know I am only one person among thousands or more that you have to look after, but to me this is both personally damaging and humiliating. You may not understand it and you don't have to--all I'm asking is that when people look at my credit file, they see the most accurate information and that's not what's happening.

Please provide me with the requested information right away so I can finally put this nightmare behind me.

I look forward to hearing from you as I am actively looking for a new job and wouldn't want these mistakes on my credit report to stand in my way.

Sincerely,

{Your signature}

{Your Printed Name}

{Your Address}

{Your Phone Number}

{Your Social Security Number}

Include a copy of the credit report showing which accounts you are disputing

Include a copy of your original letter

**Include a copy of the Bureau's response showing no changes to your

credit**

LETTER #6

(Stress letter to creditor if disputed items are still not removed)

{Name of Creditor}

{Address}

{Date}

{Name on account}

To whom it may concern:

On {Date of your first letter} I sent you a letter asking you to investigate several mistakes on my credit report. I've included a copy of my first letter and a copy of the report with the mistakes circled. According to your response you have chosen to leave these negative items on my credit report adding insult to injury. The items in question are:

{Account number 1}

{Account number 2}

{Account number 3}

I find it completely unacceptable that you and the credit bureau refuse to properly investigate my dispute. Your refusal to follow the Fair Credit Reporting Act is causing me untold stress and anxiety. Since you won't follow through, I want to know exactly how you investigated each account. Therefore I would like the <u>name, title and contact information</u> for the person at your company who did the investigation. This will allow me to personally follow up with them and find out why they are choosing to report these mistakes on my credit month after month.

I know I am only one person among thousands or more that you have to look after, but to me this is both personally damaging and humiliating. You may not understand it and you don't have to--all I'm asking is that when people look at my credit file, they see the most accurate information and that's not what's happening.

Please provide me with the requested information right away so I can finally put this nightmare behind me.

I look forward to hearing from you as I am actively looking for a new job and wouldn't want these mistakes on my credit report to stand in my way.

Sincerely,

{Your signature}

{Your Printed Name}

{Your Address}

{Your Phone Number}

{Your Social Security Number}

Include a copy of the credit report showing which accounts you are disputing

Include a copy of your original letter

Include a copy of the Bureau's response showing no changes to your credit

LETTER #7

(Threat of complaint to FTC about a credit bureau)

{Name of Credit Bureau}

{Address}

{Date}

{Name on account}

{Report Number}

To whom it may concern:

On {Date of first letter} I sent you a letter asking you to investigate several mistakes on my credit report. I've included a copy of my first letter and a copy of the report with the mistakes circled. According to your response you have chosen to leave these negative items on my credit report adding insult to injury. The items in question are:

{Original Creditor / Account number 1}

{Original Creditor / Account number 2}

{Original Creditor / Account number 3}

I realize you have a busy job and have to respond to so many of these requests, but to me this is bordering on discrimination. As a consumer I have rights and am protected by the Fair Credit Reporting Act. So far I have been very patient, but my patience has reached its limit.

If you continue to refuse to properly investigate these errors so they can be corrected, I will be forced to file a complaint with the Federal Trade Commission regarding this illegal behavior. I would much rather just deal with you, but you are leaving me no choice. It obviously doesn't bother you to report these mistakes every month, but I am being seriously damaged both monetarily and emotionally by your actions.

Please thoroughly investigate and remove these mistakes right away so I can finally put this nightmare behind me. Once you have investigated these mistakes and removed them, please send me a copy of my updated credit report.

Thank you,

{Your signature}

{Your Printed Name}

{Your Address}

{Your Phone Number}

{Your Social Security Number}

cc: Federal Trade Commission, Washington, DC

Include a copy of the credit report showing which accounts you are disputing

Include a copy of your original letter

Include a copy of the Bureau's response showing no changes to your credit

LETTER #8

(Copy of complaint to Federal Trade Commission)

{Name of Credit Bureau}

{Address}

{Date}

{Name on account}

{Report Number}

To whom it may concern:

On {Date of your first letter} I sent you a letter asking you to investigate several mistakes on my credit report. I've included a copy of my first letter and a copy of the report with the mistakes circled. Since then and in spite of my best efforts, you have chosen to leave these negative items on my credit report which is just making things worse. The items in question are:

{Original Creditor / Account number 1}

{Original Creditor / Account number 2}

{Original Creditor / Account number 3}

Since you have decided against doing your job and properly investigating these items so they can be accurately reported, I have decided to take the only recourse available to me and alert the FTC about your negligence. Included is a copy of my complaint to the FTC detailing your repeated refusal to properly report my credit history.

* * *

I will be more than happy to stop this process before a lawsuit or fines get involved, but to do that I need you to actually fully investigate these items and remove the mistakes from my credit report.

I get it--99% of these disputes are frivolous and you are right to ignore them or just pencil whip them, but that's not the case here. These negative items are NOT CORRECT and are damaging my credit worthiness costing me money, sleep and possibly my dream job.

For the last time, I am begging you to thoroughly investigate and remove these mistakes right away so I can finally put this nightmare behind me. Once you have investigated these mistakes and removed them, please send me a copy of my updated credit report.

Thank you,

{Your signature}

{Your Printed Name}

{Your Address}

{Your Phone Number}

{Your Social Security Number}

Include a copy of the credit report showing which accounts you are disputing

Include a copy of your original letter

**Include a copy of the Bureau's response showing no changes to your

credit**

Include a copy of your complaint letter to the FTC

LETTER #9

(Threat of complaint to your state's Attorney General about a creditor)

{Name of Creditor}

{Address}

{Date}

{Name on account}

To whom it may concern:

On {Date of your first letter} I sent you a letter asking you to investigate several mistakes on my credit report. I've included a copy of my first letter and a copy of the report with the mistakes circled. According to your response you have chosen to leave these negative items on my credit report adding insult to injury. The items in question are:

{Account number 1}

{Account number 2}

{Account number 3}

I realize you have a busy job and have to respond to so many of these requests, but to me this is bordering on discrimination. As a consumer I have rights and am protected by the Fair Credit Reporting Act. So far I have been very patient, but my patience has reached its limit.

If you continue to refuse to properly investigate these errors so they can be corrected, I will be forced to file a complaint with the {state name} Attorney General regarding this illegal behavior. I would much rather just deal with you, but you are leaving me no choice. It obviously doesn't bother you to report these mistakes every month, but I am being seriously damaged both monetarily and emotionally by your actions.

Please thoroughly investigate and remove these mistakes right away so I can finally put this nightmare behind me. Once you have investigated these mistakes and correctly reported them, please send me a letter confirming the changes for my records.

I apologize for being so abrasive, but this issue has gone on far too long and is a constant source of stress for me. I am in the middle of a job search and have no doubt that these mistakes on my credit report are hindering my progress. Please just do the right thing and get this negative information off my credit report.

Thank you,

{Your signature}

{Your Printed Name}

{Your Address}

{Your Phone Number}

{Your Social Security Number}

cc: Attorney General, State of {state name}

Include a copy of the credit report showing which accounts you are disputing

Include a copy of your original letter

Include a copy of the Bureau's response showing no changes to your credit

LETTER #10

(Copy of complaint to the Attorney General)

{Name of Creditor}

{Address}

{Date}

{Name on account}

To whom it may concern:

On {Date of your first letter} I sent you a letter asking you to investigate several mistakes on my credit report. I've included a copy of my first letter and a copy of the report with the mistakes circled. Since then and in spite of my best efforts, you have chosen to leave these negative items on my credit report which is just making things worse. The items in question are:

{Account number 1}

{Account number 2}

{Account number 3}

Since you have decided against doing your job and properly investigating these items so they can be accurately reported, I have decided to take the only recourse available to me and alert the Attorney General about your negligence. Included is a copy of my complaint to the Attorney General for the state of {state name} detailing your repeated refusal to properly report my credit history.

* * *

I will be more than happy to stop this process before a lawsuit or fines get involved, but to do that I need you to actually fully investigate these items and remove the mistakes from my credit report.

I get it--99% of these disputes are frivolous and you are right to ignore them or just pencil whip them, but that's not the case here. These negative items are NOT CORRECT and are damaging my credit worthiness costing me money, sleep and possibly my dream job.

For the last time, I am begging you to thoroughly investigate and remove these mistakes right away so I can finally put this nightmare behind me. Once you have investigated these mistakes and removed them, please send me a letter with the changes.

Thank you,

{Your signature}

{Your Printed Name}

{Your Address}

{Your Phone Number}

{Your Social Security Number}

Include a copy of the credit report showing which accounts you are disputing

Include a copy of your original letter

**Include a copy of the Bureau's response showing no changes to your

credit**

Include a copy of your complaint letter to the Attorney General;

LETTER #11

(Letter to Credit Bureau disputing the use of E-Oscar)

{Name of Credit Bureau}

{Address}

{Date}

{Name on account}

{Report number}

To whom it may concern:

On {Date of your first letter} I sent you a letter asking you to investigate several mistakes on my credit report. I've included a copy of my first letter and a copy of the report with the mistakes circled. Over the past several months, in spite of my efforts you have chosen not to properly investigate and correct these items. The items in question are:

{Creditor 1 / Account number}

{Creditor 2 / Account number}

{Creditor 3 / Account number}

I find it completely unbelievable that you and the creditor refuse to properly investigate my dispute and for the longest time I could not begin to understand why. Upon doing some research on how credit bureaus work, I discovered something very disturbing. Due to the volume of disputes you receive, you are having a computer read my letters and electronically respond to them.

To think that while I sit out here suffering from these mistakes on my credit report, some computer at your company is merely exchanging information with a computer at my creditor. Quite obviously if the creditor's computer had the correct information I wouldn't be in this situation. Therefore, I find it totally unacceptable that you would ask that same mistake-prone computer to verify the accuracy of my account. No wonder I've been beating my head against this wall for so long!!

You are bound to investigate each dispute fully and accurately by law. You are not however bound to use a computer to computer method to do so. I am now officially asking you to use human beings to contact other human beings at my creditors so perhaps you can all figure out what I already know--these mistakes on my credit shouldn't be there.

By law, you have 30 days to complete this process. I expect to hear from someone--not a computer--some time in the next 30 days with the results of the *human* investigation into these mistakes on my credit report.

Please provide me an updated copy of my credit report along with the names and contact information of the people involved with my investigation.

Sincerely,

{Your signature}

{Your Printed Name}

{Your Address}

{Your Phone Number}

{Your Social Security Number}

Include a copy of the credit report showing which accounts you are disputing

Include a copy of your original letter

Include a copy of the Bureau's response showing no changes to your credit

LETTER #12

(Cash for negative items removal from Creditor)

{Name of Creditor}

{Address}

{Date}

{Name on account}

To whom it may concern:

On {Date of your credit report}, I received a copy of my credit report and it shows my account number {account number} with you as delinquent. I have attempted numerous times to get this negative information corrected on my credit report and as yet, have been unsuccessful. At the moment, I am under the gun with both a job search and potential home purchase and just need to get these items off my credit report.

Therefore, I propose that we reach an agreement that is mutually beneficial:

I will make a lump sum payment of ${amount offered} and your company agrees to immediately and permanently remove the negative information from my credit file associated with this account.

If my offer is acceptable to you, please confirm by signing the acceptance below and returning this letter to me in the enclosed envelope.

* * *

Sincerely,

{Your signature}

{Your Printed Name}

{Your Address}

{Your Phone Number}

Agreed to and accepted on this _______ day of __________________, 20_____.

By: ____

Printed name: ________________________________

Title: _______________________________________

Include a copy of the credit report showing which accounts you are referring to

CHAPTER EIGHT

Fair Credit Reporting Act (FCRA)

From Wikipedia, the free encyclopedia

The **Fair Credit Reporting Act**, 15 U.S.C. § 1681 ("**FCRA**") is U.S. Federal Government legislation enacted to promote the accuracy, fairness, and privacy of consumer information contained in the files of consumer reporting agencies. It was intended to protect consumers from the willful and/or negligent inclusion of inaccurate information in their credit reports. To that end, the FCRA regulates the collection, dissemination, and use of consumer information, including consumer credit information.[1] Together with the Fair Debt Collection Practices Act ("FDCPA"), the FCRA forms the foundation of consumer rights law in the United States. It was originally passed in 1970,[2] and is enforced by the US Federal Trade Commission, the Consumer Financial Protection Bureau and private litigants.

Contents

· 11) External Links

History

The Fair Credit Reporting Act, as originally enacted, was title VI of Pub.L. 91–508, 84 Stat. 1114, enacted October 26, 1970, entitled *An Act to amend the Federal Deposit Insurance Act to require insured banks to maintain certain records, to require that certain transactions in United States currency be reported to the Department of the Treasury, and for other purposes*. It was written as an amendment to add a title VI to the Consumer Credit Protection Act, Pub.L. 90–321, 82 Stat. 146, enacted June 29, 1968.

Consumer reports

Commonly referred to as credit reports, a consumer report "contains information about your credit - and some bill repayment history - and the status of your credit accounts. This information includes how often you make your payments on time, how much credit you have, how much credit you have available, how much credit you are using, and whether a debt or bill collector is collecting on money you owe. Credit reports also can contain rental repayment information if you are a property renter. It also can contain public records such as liens, judgments, and bankruptcies that provide insight into your financial status and obligations."[3]

Inaccuracies in consumer reports

A 2015 study released by the Federal Trade Commission found that 23% of consumers identified inaccurate information in their credit reports.[4] Under the Fair and Accurately reflect Credit Transactions Act (FACTA), an amendment to the FCRA passed in 2003, consumers are able to receive a free copy of their consumer report from each credit reporting agency once a year.[5] The free report can be requested by telephone, mail, or through the government-authorized website: annualcreditreport.com.[6] Consumer reports obtained through annualcreditreport.com make it easy to identify and dispute inaccurate information.

Civil liability

The FCRA regulates:

1. Consumer reporting agencies;
2. Users of consumer reports; and,

3. Furnishers of consumer information.

If a consumer's rights under the FCRA are violated, they can recover:

1. Actual or statutory damages;
2. Attorney's fees;
3. Court costs; and,
4. Punitive damages if the violation was wilful.[7] "The threat of punitive damages under 1681n of the FCRA is the primary factor deterring erroneous reporting by the reporting industry."[8]

The statute of limitations requires consumers to file suit prior to the earlier of: two years after the violation is discovered; or, five years after the violation occurred.[7]

Consumer attorneys often take these cases on a contingency fee basis because the statute allows a consumer to recover attorney's fees from the offending party.

Users of consumer reports

Users of the information for credit, insurance, or employment purposes (including background checks) have the following responsibilities under the FCRA:

1. Users can only obtain consumer reports for permissible purposes under the FCRA;
2. Users must notify the consumer when an adverse action is taken on the basis of such reports; and,
3. Users must identify the company that provided the report, so that the accuracy and completeness of the report may be verified or contested by the consumer.

Employment background checks

Employers using consumer reports to screen job applicants or employees must follow specific procedures:

1. Get your written permission;
2. Tell you how they want to use your credit report;
3. Not misuse your information;
4. Give you a copy of your credit report if the employer decides not to hire or fires you; and,
5. Give you an opportunity to dispute the information contained within your credit report before making a final adverse decision.[9]

Furnishers of information

A creditor, as defined by the FCRA, is a company that furnishes information to consumer reporting agencies. Typically, these are creditors, with which a consumer has some sort of credit agreement (such as credit card companies, auto finance companies and mortgage banking institutions).

Other examples of information furnishers are collection agencies (third-party collectors), state or municipal courts reporting a judgment of some kind, past and present employers and bonders. Lenders have an important role to play in ensuring credit reports are accurate. Under the FCRA, creditors who furnish information about consumers to consumer reporting agencies must:[10]

1. Provide complete and accurate information to the credit reporting agencies;
2. Investigate consumer disputes received from credit reporting agencies;
3. Correct, delete, or verify information within 30 days of receipt of a dispute; and,
4. Inform consumers about negative information which is in the process of or has already been placed on a consumer's credit report within one month.

(This notice doesn't have to be sent as a separate notice, but may be placed on a consumer's monthly statement. If sent as part as the monthly statement, it needs to be conspicuous, but need not be in bold type. Required wording (developed by the US Federal Treasury Department):

Notice before negative information is reported: *We may report information about your account to credit bureaus. Late payments, missed payments, or other defaults on your account may be reflected in your credit report.*

Notice after negative information is reported: *We have told a credit bureau about a late payment, missed payment or other default on your account. This information may be reflected in your credit report.*

Consumer reporting agencies ("CRAs")

Consumer reporting agencies (CRAs) are entities that collect and disseminate information about consumers to be used for credit evaluation and certain other purposes, including employment. Credit bureaus, a type of consumer reporting agency, hold a consumer's credit report in their databases. CRAs have a number of responsibilities under FCRA, including the following:

1. CRAs must maintain reasonable procedures to ensure the

maximum possible accuracy of the information contained within a consumer's report;[7]

2. Provide a consumer with information about him or her in the agency's files and take steps to verify the accuracy of information disputed by a consumer;

3. If negative information is removed as a result of a consumer's dispute, it may not be reinserted without notifying the consumer in writing within five days; and,

4. Remove negative information seven years after the date of first delinquency (except for bankruptcies (10 years) and tax liens (seven years from the time they are paid).

The three big CRAs—Experian, TransUnion, and Equifax—do not interact with information furnishers directly as a result of consumer disputes. They use a system called E-Oscar.[11] In some areas of the country, however, there are other credit bureaus.

Nationwide specialty consumer reporting agencies

In addition to the three big CRAs, the FCRA also classifies dozens of other information technology companies as "nationwide specialty consumer reporting agencies" that produce individual consumer reports used to make credit determinations.[12] Under Section 603 of the Fair Credit Reporting Act, the term "nationwide specialty consumer reporting agency" means a consumer reporting agency that compiles and maintains files on consumers on a nationwide basis relating to:

1. Medical records or payments;
2. Residential or tenant history;
3. Check writing history;
4. Criminal background; and,
5. Other public record information.

Because these nationwide specialty consumer reporting agencies sell consumer credit report files, they are required to provide annual disclosures of their report files to any consumer who requests disclosure.[13] A partial list of companies classified as nationwide specialty consumer reporting agencies under FCRA includes: Telecheck, ChoicePoint, Acxiom, Integrated Screening Partners, Innovis, the Insurance Services Office, Tenant Data Services, LexisNexis, Retail Equation, Central Credit, Teletrack, the MIB Group, United Health Group (Ingenix Division), and Milliman.[14]

Although the major CRAs Experian, Equifax, and TransUnion are required by law to provide a central source website for consumers to request their reports, the nationwide specialty consumer reporting agencies are not required to provide a centralized online source for disclosure. The FCRA Section 612 merely requires nationwide specialty consumer reporting agencies to establish a streamlined process for consumers to request consumer reports, which shall include, at a minimum, the establishment by each such agency of a toll-free telephone number for such consumer disclosure requests.[12]

See also

· annualcreditreport.com
· Adverse Credit History
· Background check
· Credit card
· Credit history
· Credit rating agency
· Credit score
· Fair and Accurate Credit Transactions Act
· Fair Credit Billing Act
· Identity theft
· Identity Theft Resource Center
· Political and Economic Research Council—think tank who did much of the research for FCRA reauthorization
· Tenant Screening

References

1. *Dlabay, Les R.; Burrow, James L.; Brad, Brad (2009). Intro to Business. Mason, Ohio: South-Western Cengage Learning. p. 471. ISBN 978-0-538-44561-0.*

2. *"Budgeting Tools". Money Management. Retrieved 2 October 2012.*

3. *"What is a credit report?". Consumerfinance.gov. Consumer Financial Protection Bureau. February 27, 2014. Retrieved October 15, 2015.*

4. *"Report to Congress Under Section 319 of the Fair and Accurate Credit Transactions Act of 2003" (PDF). www.ftc.gov. Federal Trade Commission. December 2012. Retrieved October 16, 2015.*

5. *"Provisions of New Fair and Accurate Credit Transactions Act Will Help Reduce Identity Theft and Help Victims Recover: FTC". Ftc.gov. 2011-06-24. Retrieved 2012-10-02.*

6. http://www.consumer.ftc.gov/articles/0155-free-credit-reports

7. *"The Fair Credit Reporting Act" (PDF). www.consumer.ftc.gov. Federal*

Trade Commission. Retrieved October 15, 2015.

8. *"Brim V. Midland Credit Mgmt. Inc., 795 F.Supp.2d 1255 (N.D. Ala. 2011)". Casetext.com. United States District Court for the Northern District of Alabama. 2011. Retrieved October 15, 2015.*

9. *"Employment Background Checks". Consumer.ftc.gov. Federal Trade Commission. November 2014. Retrieved October 15, 2015.*

10. *"WILLIAMS: Credit agencies are the messengers". Washington Times. 2009-01-19. Retrieved 2012-10-02.*

11. *"Home". E-Oscar. Retrieved 2012-10-02.*

12. *"Text of the Fair Credit Reporting Act, 15 U.S.C. 1681" (PDF). Ftc.gov. Retrieved 2012-10-02.*

13. [1]

14. *"Do a Total Background Check on Yourself - Annual Consumer Reporting Agencies". AnnualMedicalReport.com. Retrieved 2012-10-02.*

CHAPTER NINE

Your rights under the FCRA

A Summary of Your Rights Under the Fair Credit Reporting Act

The federal Fair Credit Reporting Act (FCRA) promotes the accuracy, fairness, and privacy of information in the files of consumer reporting agencies. There are many types of consumer reporting agencies, including credit bureaus and specialty agencies (such as agencies that sell information about check writing histories, medical records, and rental history records). Here is a summary of your major rights under the FCRA.

For more information, including information about additional rights, go

to www.ftc.gov/credit

Or write to:

Consumer Response Center
Room 130-A
Federal Trade Commission
600 Pennsylvania Ave. N.W.
Washington, D.C. 20580.

You must be told if information in your file has been used against you.

Anyone who uses a credit report or another type of consumer report to deny your application for credit, insurance, or employment – or to take another adverse action against you – must tell you, and must give you the name, address, and phone number of the agency that provided the information.

You have the right to know what is in your file.

You may request and obtain all the information about you in the files of a consumer reporting agency (your "file disclosure"). You will be required to provide proper identification, which may include your Social Security number. In many cases, the disclosure will be free.

You are entitled to a free file disclosure if:

- a person has taken adverse action against you because of information in your credit report
- you are the victim of identify theft and place a fraud alert in your file
- your file contains inaccurate information as a result of fraud
- you are on public assistance
- you are unemployed but expect to apply for employment within 60 days.

In addition, by September 2005 all consumers will be entitled to one free disclosure every 12 months upon request from each nationwide credit bureau and from nationwide specialty consumer reporting agencies. See www.ftc.gov/credit for additional information.

You have the right to ask for a credit score.

Credit scores are numerical summaries of your credit-worthiness based on information from credit bureaus. You may request a credit score from consumer reporting agencies that create scores or distribute scores used in residential real property loans, but you will have to pay for it. In some mortgage transactions, you will receive credit score information for free from the mortgage lender.

You have the right to dispute incomplete or inaccurate information.

If you identify information in your file that is incomplete or inaccurate, and report it to the consumer reporting agency, the agency must investigate unless your dispute is frivolous. See www.ftc.gov/credit for an explanation of dispute procedures.

Consumer reporting agencies must correct or delete inaccurate, incomplete, or

unverifiable information.

Inaccurate, incomplete or unverifiable information must be removed or corrected, usually within 30 days. However, a consumer reporting agency may continue to report information it has verified as accurate.

Consumer reporting agencies may not report outdated negative information.

In most cases, a consumer reporting agency may not report negative information that is more than seven years old, or bankruptcies that are more than 10 years old.

Access to your file is limited.

A consumer reporting agency may provide information about you only to people with a valid need -- usually to consider an application with a creditor, insurer, employer, landlord, or other business. The FCRA specifies those with a valid need for access.

You must give your consent for reports to be provided to employers.

A consumer reporting agency may not give out information about you to your employer, or a potential employer, without your written consent given to the employer. Written consent generally is not required in the trucking industry. For more information,

go to www.ftc.gov/credit.

You may limit "prescreened" offers of credit and insurance you get based on information in your credit report.

Unsolicited "prescreened" offers for credit and insurance must include a toll-free phone number you can call if you choose to remove your name and address from the lists these offers are based on. You may opt-out with the nationwide credit bureaus at

1-888-5-OPTOUT (1-888-567-8688).

You may seek damages from violators.

If a consumer reporting agency, or, in some cases, a user of consumer reports or a furnisher of information to a consumer reporting agency violates the FCRA, you may be able to sue in state or federal court.

Identity theft victims and active duty military personnel have additional rights.

For more information, visit www.ftc.gov/credit.

* * *

States may enforce the FCRA, and many states have their own consumer reporting laws.

In some cases, you may have more rights under state law. For more information, contact your state or local consumer protection agency or your state Attorney General.

CHAPTER TEN

Government contacts

TYPE OF BUSINESS:	**CONTACT:**
Consumer reporting agencies, creditors and others not listed below	Federal Trade Commission Consumer Response Center 600 Pennsylvania Ave., NW Washington, DC 20580 www.ftccomplaintassistant.gov 877-382-4357
National banks, federal branches/agencies of foreign banks (word "National" or initials "N.A." appear in or after bank's name)	Office of the Comptroller of the Currency Compliance Management Washington, DC 20219 www.occ.treas.gov 800-613-6743
Federal Reserve System member banks (except national banks, and federal branches/agencies of foreign banks)	Federal Reserve Consumer Help P O Box 1200 Minneapolis, MN 55480 www.federalreserveconsumerhelp.gov

* * *	ConsumerHelp@FederalReserve.gov 888-851-1920
Savings associations and federally chartered savings banks (word "Federal" or initials "F.S.B." appear in federal institution's name)	Office of Thrift Supervision Consumer Complaints Washington, DC 20552 www.treasury.gov/about/history/pages/ots.aspx 800-842-6929
Federal credit unions (words "Federal Credit Union" appear in institution's name)	National Credit Union Administration 1775 Duke Street Alexandria, VA 22314 www.ncua.gov 703-519-4600
State-chartered banks that are not members of the Federal Reserve System	Federal Deposit Insurance Corporation Consumer Response Center, 2345 Grand Avenue, Suite 100 Kansas City, Missouri 64108-2638 www.fdic.gov 877-275-3342
Air, surface, or rail common carriers regulated by former Civil Aeronautics Board or Interstate Commerce Commission	Department of Transportation Office of Financial Management Washington, DC 20590 www.transportation.gov 202-366-1306

Made in the USA
Las Vegas, NV
02 July 2021

25833404R00046